Charles Drew

Doctor

Written by Garnet Nelson Jackson
Illustrated by Gary Thomas

MODERN CURRICULUM PRESS

Program Reviewers

Leila Eames, Coordinator of Instruction,
    Chapter 1
    New Orleans Public Schools
    New Orleans, Louisiana

Stephanie Mahan, Teacher
    Bethune Elementary School
    San Diego, California

Thomasina M. Portis, Director
    Multicultural/Values Education
    District of Columbia
    Public Schools
    Washington, D.C.

MODERN CURRICULUM PRESS

13900 Prospect Road, Cleveland, Ohio 44136

A Paramount Publishing Company

ISBN 0-8136-5238-3 (Reinforced Binding)   0-8136-5244-8 (Paperback)

Library of Congress Catalog Card Number: 93-79427

Dear Readers,

Charles Drew was always a winner. Even as a young boy, he showed special talents and won regularly.

Usually a person with special talents has to practice and practice in order to win. This is how it was with Charles. He put in many hours of hard work.

Because Charles believed in "never giving up," he made a discovery that saved many lives.

We too, should practice and study at whatever we decide to do in life.

Your friend,

Garnet Jackson

Speedy arms and legs cut through the water. The splashing almost hid the tiny swimmer.

He was one of the best, above all the rest!

Charles Drew was one of the youngest swimmers. Even so, he won the neighborhood swimming contest. This was his first victory. There were many more victories to come.

Through thick and thin, he would always win.

4

Charles was the oldest of Richard and Nora Drew's five children. His brothers and sisters all looked up to him.

In his Washington, D.C. school, Charles was a star in baseball, track, football, and basketball. Most of his friends and family thought he would earn his living as an athlete. But Charles liked to study as well as play sports. When he graduated from high school, he decided to become a doctor.

He was still the champ in his camp.

In 1922, Charles went to Amherst College in Massachusetts. Again he proved he was a great athlete. More important, he did well in his classes, too. By the time he graduated, he had been awarded many honors and prizes.

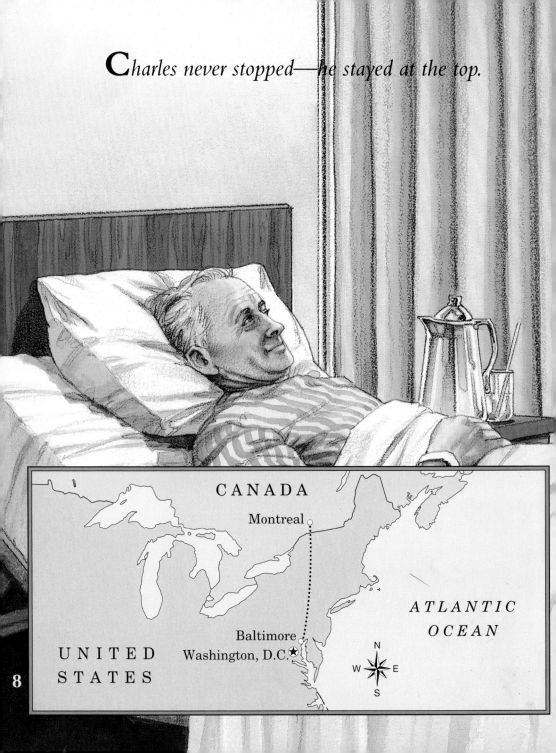

Charles never stopped—he stayed at the top.

CANADA

Montreal

UNITED
STATES

Baltimore
Washington, D.C.

ATLANTIC
OCEAN

N
W · E
S

8

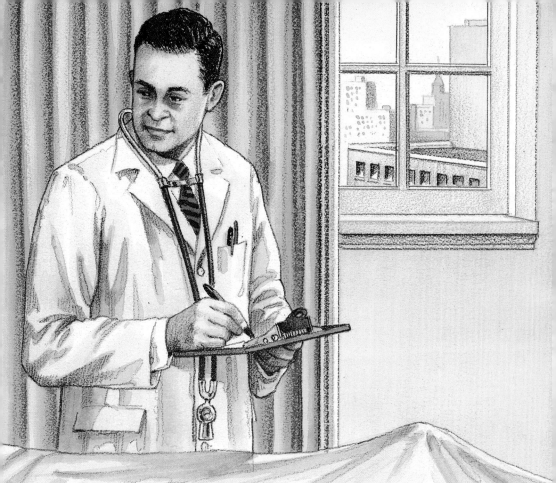

Charles went to Montreal, Canada, to study medicine at McGill University. He was one of the best students in his class. After years of study, Charles became a doctor.

Everyone knew what Charles could do.

Charles wanted to learn more about the blood in people's bodies. He worked very hard studying blood and how it worked.

Charles also became a surgeon. He performed many operations. Often he saw that people needed to be given extra blood to keep them alive.

11

It was possible for people to donate blood for operations. Hospitals tried to keep this blood on hand for people who would need it. But doctors did not know how to keep the blood fresh. They could not be sure there would always be blood when it was needed.

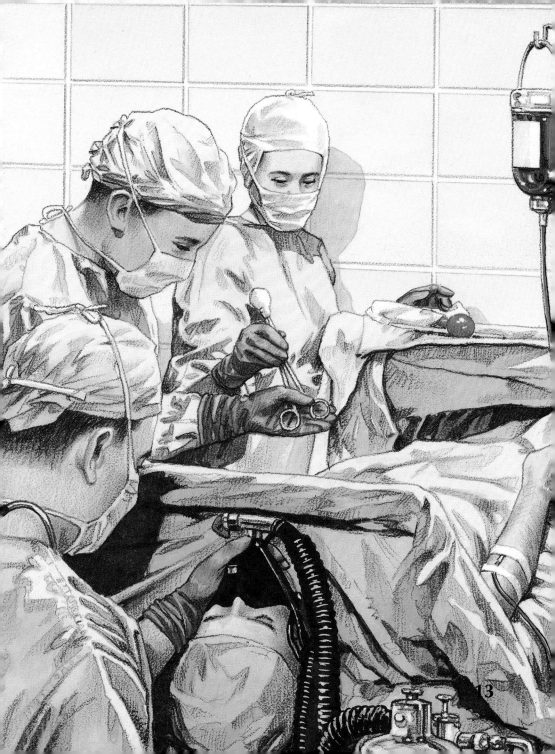

13

Dr. *Drew to the rescue!*

Charles thought about the problem and tried different experiments to solve it. Then he made a discovery.

The watery part of blood is called plasma. Charles discovered a way to separate plasma from the rest of the blood. He found that plasma could be kept fresh for a long time. Doctors could use plasma in place of whole blood.

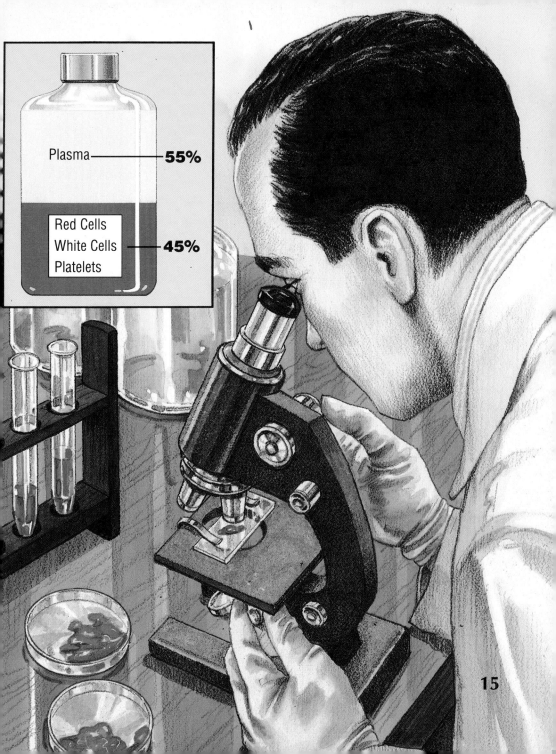

Plasma — **55%**

Red Cells
White Cells — **45%**
Platelets

15

Their request was for the best.

ENGLAND

London

UNITED
STATES

ATLANTIC

OCEAN

N
W E
S

16

Charles became famous all over the world for this great discovery. In 1939 a huge war began—World War II. Many people were hurt. Doctors needed plasma to keep people alive. Doctors in England asked Charles to help them.

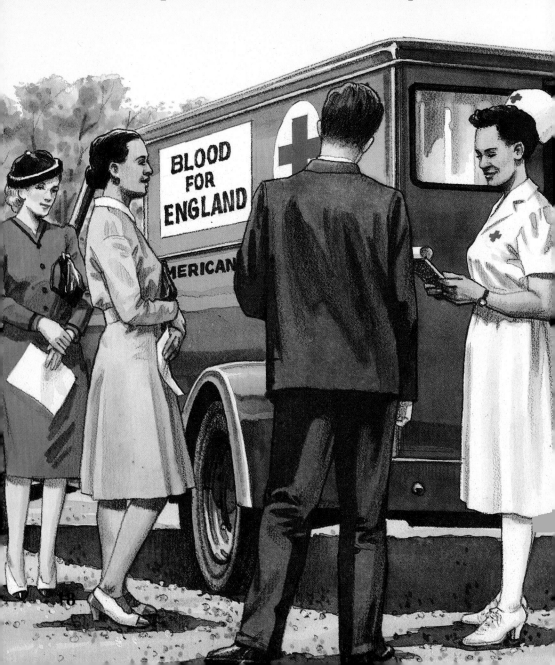

When put to the test, Drew was truly the best.

England needed large supplies of plasma for wounded people. Charles's teams of doctors and nurses collected blood from people in America. They stored the blood in refrigerators. Places where blood was stored were called "Blood Banks."

Charles's teams separated the plasma out of the blood. Then they sent the plasma to England.

20

21

Charles saved many lives in England. Later his blood banks saved many Americans. Charles was famous and admired the world over.

Charles became a teacher at a school for doctors. He taught at Howard University, an African American college in his hometown.

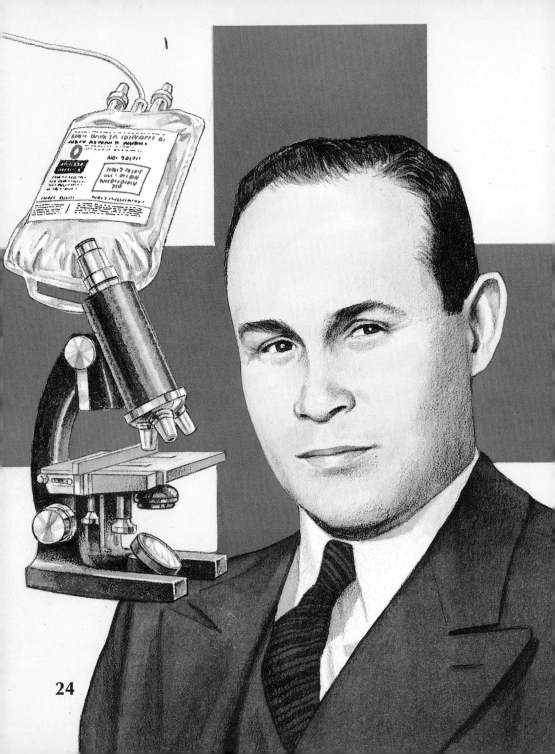

Sometimes people still need blood to save their lives. Now they can get the blood they need. Stored blood saves many lives, thanks to Dr. Charles Drew.

Glossary

collect (kə lekt') To bring things together

donate (dō' nāt) To give in order to help others

graduate (graj' ōo wāt) To leave a school because studies are finished

operation (äp' ə rā' shən) An action taken by a doctor to fix a body part. Usually the doctor uses tools and cuts into the body.

plasma (plaz' mə) The watery part of blood

separate (sep' ə rāt) To divide into parts or groups

surgeon (sʉr' jən) A doctor who does operations

victory (vik' tə rē) A win

About the Author

Garnet Jackson was born and raised in New Orleans, Louisiana. She is now an elementary school teacher in Flint, Michigan, with a deep concern for developing a positive self-image in young African American students. After an unsuccessful search for materials on famous African Americans written for early readers, Ms. Jackson produced a series of biographies herself. She has now written a second series. Besides being a teacher, Ms. Jackson is a poet and a newspaper columnist. She dedicates this book with love to her son Damon.

About the Illustrator

Gary Thomas, a native of Ohio, has worked as a commercial illustrator for over thirty years. His distinctive, photo-realistic style can be seen in many illustrations in the U.S. Olympic, Pro Football, and Bowling Halls of Fame. In *Charles Drew*, Thomas uses water-color and colored pencil to present Drew's personal and professional experiences with detailed accuracy.